The inspiration to write began when I first met my ⎯⎯⎯⎯⎯⎯⎯
back in 1965. I wrote lots of poems to her in an ⎯⎯⎯⎯⎯⎯⎯, it worked!
We married in 1966, and quite often over the years that followed she would say,
'Why don't you write poetry anymore?'

The truth is that I seldom had any spare time, with working, rearing a family, and building a business. Following her death in 2022, grief inspired me to resume writing again, both as a tribute to her, but also as an outlet for my pain, which I know many struggle to come to terms with.

There are many poems in this book which are clearly linked to Cathy, but the desire to write others of a more light hearted nature will hopefully show the benefits of writing to relieve the pain of grief, hence the title,

POEMS TO REFRESH THE SOUL
By David Roper

Acknowledgements

I would like to thank Cathy's niece Monika for editorial advice from Ireland, my daughters Bernadette and Maggie for encouragement and their love of my poems, and my daughter Alison for her work bringing the book to print

DESERVING

You deserve all the sunbeams
That scatter around,
You deserve all the flowers
That spring from the ground ,
You deserve all the stars
That glisten and twinkle,
You deserve all the raindrops
That from heaven do sprinkle,
You deserve all the moonbeams
From heaven unfurled,
Just the same way
That you lit up my world!

WHAT IF

What if…
The sky was pink
The trees all black
The grass an awful grey,
Would it still be real
Like any other day?

What if, what if
It had never come to be
That our world was as it is,
Could we sit so easily?

What if, what if
It was not just as it seems,
And when we thought the lights went out
It was just another dream.

THE GRAVEYARD

There is no malice in the graveyard
No animosity,
Just peace and bird song chatter
There is no malice here.
Nothing here to matter
All troubles left outside
Think of all the souls
That walked these paths before
All the worries that they had
Are left at heavens door,
For no matter how they tried
There was no peace before.
No malice in the graveyard
No fear of any hate
No malice in the peaceful calm,
Just the squeaking of the gate.

Enter now another soul
To join those resting here,
Who rest in silence all around
Away from noise and rush,
With the birds which live here
Blackbird, sparrow, thrush;
And don't forget the robin,
With its little bib of red,
Skillfully building up his nest
So like the others(lying here)
Can rest its weary head.

The trees stand guard all around
Ash willow, beech and yew,
That are the home for squirrels
Rabbits, foxes, other creatures too,
No malice in this graveyard
The life that lives here thrives,
Constantly watching over you,
So rest in peace, and be assured
For all that life has now passed by,
There is no malice here.

OBSERVING

I gazed upon the headstones
At names, called before their time,
Up to now, thankfully
None of them is mine!

EVOLUTION

Time it is invisible, to our human eye
Yet it comes and passes
And we know not why,
Why does it go so quickly
For things we most enjoy?
But seems to last forever
The things which make us cry!

Time it is perpetual
Something we can't change.
Along the winding corridor
We travel, to the end,
Our time we must not waste it
As destiny we follow,
Evolution to transcend.

YESTERDAY, TODAY, TOMORROW

Today, as yesterday
Is filled with sadness and sorrow
For I miss you so much
Yesterday, today, and tomorrow.

For it seems since you went
Blackness fills each day
Each hour is only spent
Thinking of yesterday, not today, or tomorrow.

So, it is with gratitude
Being grateful for what I had,
I take a positive attitude
to yesterday, today, and perhaps tomorrow.

SHARING

That lovely sunset,
Which you so much enjoyed
Means nothing, without you
Being here to share.

Life's journey carries on
With all it's ups and downs
Its joys, its worries,
All are nothing
If you're not here to share.

A thousand people there could be,
Again and many more
Still I'd be all alone,
Without you here to share.

ONWARD

This world is not alone
The galaxies are vast,
Time spent here is very brief
And never meant to last.

So we must not doubt of heaven,
We know it must be there
Just exactly where it is
I neither know nor care.

What matters is, we believe it,
The bible tells us so,
There are many rooms to visit
And we have to go.

To think this world is all there is
Is not to think things through,
When this short life is over
We start the process to renew.

NOCTURNAL

The swirling mists around the trees
Make shadows fall around,
Gently springs the moonlight
To light up the frosty ground.

Creeping shadows forming
Shrill noises pierce the night,
The haunting sounds come zooming
To fill the soul with fright.

Still deeper yet the darkness,
As clouds go rolling by
Foxes bark, the owls they screech,
And bats dart round the sky.

A winter night, like magic
Transforms the daytime scene,
With harmony, an urgent call
Of things that might have been.

However cold, however bleak
The night it comes alive
To them it is but nature
They need it so, to thrive.

The wind still shrieks it's lonely cry
As daytime starts to peep,
So creatures that have been about
Lie down and start to sleep.

DREAMING OF YOU

I dreamed a dream
And it came true
I dreamed a dream
And it was you!

Life can be strange,
I know that's true
But out of nowhere
Came little ole you!

MYSTERY

Through avenues of darkness
Lie cul de sacs of fear
And a sense of foreboding,
With danger ever near.

Through swirling mists of make believe
Are temptations of the mind,
That deceive us into thinking
We can leave it all behind.

Through mountains of great darkness
Reaching for the sky,
To valleys of lush greenery,
That leaves us wondering why.

From the forests and the hillsides
That descend into the sea
All will one day crumble,
Just as sure as we.

THE EAGLE'S EYE

From way up high the eagle flies
It's hapless prey to seek,
Gracefully gliding in the sky
Beware that killer beak,
They hunt without a sound ,
Descending in a streak.

The victim spotted is unaware,
No chance to make a break,
Nor find a place to hide
For them, the game is over
The hunter swoops with grace
Supper it has spied!

Gracefully, this majestic bird
Kills only to survive,
Taking just what it needs
To keep its brood alive,
Part of the great circle
Of life's eternal drive.

SOLITUDE

Solitude, I know that town
A place I've seen before
Visited it so many times
My name is on the door.

'Tis not a place wherein to dwell
Just somewhere, sometimes to go,
To contemplate life's mysteries
And why it happens so.

Wonder, as I do
Why it is we're here
Dispel, perhaps the mystery
Which fills us all with fear.

Solitude, I know that place
Somewhere, not too unkind
Just a while in time and space,
To refresh the soul and mind.

Solitude, a welcome time
Reflecting as we should,
On things we haven't done,
And maybe never could.

Solitude, just to be alone
Within your mortal soul
To reflect, and think about
In life, what is my goal?

A NEW YEAR

New year dawns, another chance
To seek old friends and new
Once again to contemplate
Decisions to review.

It maybe just a date,
But it is another chance,
To look at life differently
A brand new jig to dance.

A WINTER GARDEN

The picture of a winter garden
When it has lost its summer glow,
Fallen leaves with naked trees,
And no growing grass to mow.

Cold and uninviting,
Quiet and unexciting,
Birds and squirrels search the ground,
For any morsels to be found.

Days grow short, the wind it moans
Blowing nuts and berries, fruits and cones.
The nights are long and Jack Frost creeps
Covering all, while the garden sleeps.

All colour gone, no longer green,
But dressed in frost, an enchanting scene.

From winter's garden, nature's rise is amazing
We look with awe, like a night star gazing.
Without our help, be assured it will bring
A renewed garden that awakes each spring.
Seeds that were dormont in the soil push through,
Birdsongs and colours surround anew.

All things will pass, but don't miss the glory,
Or wondrous beauty of the winter garden story.

SPECIAL

Since the day I first saw you
I just have to say,
You brightened my night time,
And lit up my day.

Each day it was special,
You made me feel good
With each smile that you gave me,
As I knew that it would.

From when I first saw you
I knew that for sure,
I needed you always
Then, now and evermore.

REMEMBERING YOU

To hear your voice again
To touch and hold your hand
To see you like I knew you,
Now wouldn't that be grand.

To see again your smiling face
To walk with you once more
To feel again your warm embrace,
Now wouldn't that be grand.

Someone fun to walk with
To stroll along the sand
With a day beside the sea,
Now wouldn't that be grand.

To think of all the happy times
The best that we can do
Is to remember with much love,
Just as I remember you.

Although I cannot touch you
Or hear your laugh again
You are still here beside me,
That's what makes life grand.

.

HEAVEN SENT

God lent me an angel
To spend some time with me
To guide me and to love me
Trouble is you see,
What's loaned is not forever
And must go back to be
An angel up in heaven,
Hopefully waiting there, for me.

Heaven sent me an angel
To spend some time with me
To comfort and to love me
With care and tenderness,
Support and to surprise me
And help in every way,
Until the day it dawned
When she had to go away.

I cannot be ungrateful
What a treasure to have had,
An angel loaned from heaven
To help through good or bad,
How privileged, how gracious
How could I e're be sad
She changed my life forever,
What a companion to have had!

ALONE

Why I often wonder,
Did you have to go
And leave me so alone?
But, of course I know
You really had no choice
Your time to leave had come,
Now your pain has ended, hopefully.
But mine, it's just begun.

THE MIRROR

When I look into the mirror
It's very strange to see
An old man with white hair
Staring back at me.

This old man I'm thinking
I wonder who is he?
Staring out the mirror
Looking straight at me.

I wonder where he came from
A cheek, I think you might agree
To get inside my mirror
And stare right back at me!

ENLIGHTENED

When you came into my life
So unexpectedly
You lifted all the gloom
Your smile,
So wonderful to see.

When you came into my world
All changed,
Then you gave me a purpose
For everything,
All things re-arranged.

A reason to get up each day
Bringing all fresh hope,
Everything had a purpose
Looking forward
Never to look back.

You lit up all dark corners
With joy,
You gave all you could give
Brightness, hope and fun
Most of all, you gave love
To me, not everyone!

WATER OF LIFE

Cascading water, every day
Swept under the bridge
And far away,
Far as any eye can see,
Down the valley
And into the sea.

Just as life, it ebbs and flows
As everyone surely knows,
When it's gone
It can't come back,
Down the valley
Washed away its track.

Cannot return whence it came
Nor be re-invented
With a different name.
It is for some, though not all
A raging torrent
That can make us fall.

So the rush of all life's ills
Down the valley
And over the hills,
Try to find out, where it went
No chance there,
Our time is spent.

THE LAST DANCE

Oh, to have again the chance
To take you to a country dance,
Something you had loved to do,
But I was shy, clumsy too.
So, except for our wedding day,
Your wish to dance was sent away.
So to remind me, I was wrong
Your requiem contained a song,
So *"Save The Last Dance For Me"*
Became an epitaph you see,
But our life was much romance
With love and laughter, we did dance.

THINKING

Thinking, thinking, always thinking
My mind is full of this, and that
Much time to reflect
And maybe, to reject
The things we expect
To be a problem,
And to expand
On what maybe,
Just too grand,
So reject it
Out of hand.

To regurgitate a thought,
Chew it over
So to speak,
Until at last
What it is we seek,
Like a mirage, in the heat
Becomes reality
To build on,
Enthusiastically
To fruition, a rendition
Of all of life's ambition.

MOURNING

No more to see your sweet face
But I will not mourn you.
No more to feel your warm embrace
But I will not mourn you.
No more to touch your hand again
But I will not mourn you.
No more to walk the park in rain
But I will not mourn you.
No more to kiss and hold you tight
But I will not mourn you.
No more to say a fond goodnight
But still I will not mourn you,
For to mourn would be to admit
That I have lost the will,
But you know, as I should,
You are with me, still.

ALIENS VISIT

A traveller from outer space
Set out to view the human race,
He found out to his great surprise,
We appear unable to survive,
For, what the traveller, he could see
Was human extinction activity.
Destruction was at every turn,
Hatred, death, a bleaker scene
Now all black, instead of green.
So he made a hasty retreat
His elders back at home to meet,
To tell them all, while you can
Don't go near the place of man,
For their mission, as he said
Seems to wish themselves all dead.
Conclusion reached , they agreed
Earth is just too full of greed.
So reluctantly they changed the plan
For a package tour of MAN.
So, instead they viewed the stars
Then went back home, to MARS.

WHERE, I WONDER?

If I can't be here
I must be there,
But if not there
Then I must be, where?
Oft I think, oft I ponder
If I'm not here
I must be yonder.
Then begs the question
Of where I went,
And did I go
Or was I sent?
These, and many more
Seldom get beyond "what for?"
Our destiny remains a mystery,
So the question, throughout history
Remains the same, in all but name
If I'm not here
I must be THERE!

JOURNEYING

Begin with the beginning
Don't start at the end,
If you start in the middle
You'll go round the bend.
Don't go the wrong way
Up a one way street
Because If you do so
A collision you'll meet.
Don't do things in half measure,
Or give in to pressure,
Don't take a shortcut
Unless you know where,
For certain it'll lead you
To lose a fair share
Of things that give pleasure.
So don't jump the queue,
Or well you might get
Something surprising,
Your biggest shock yet.

WEASEL AND THE TOAD

No doubt you've heard all about
The race 'twixt tortoise and the hare,
But did you hear, I wonder
About the weasel and the toad?
The former ran across the field
The latter down the road.
Now that may well be faster,
But hazards there are found,
The toad, he got squashed
And the weasel went aground.
That wasn't to be expected
Wasn't very fair,
But the weasel came unstuck
When brer fox came out his lair,
And so the fox enjoyed
An unexpected brunch,
And then a little nap,
Fast asleep he went
When a pack of hungry hounds
They found him
And ate him up for lunch!

The moral of the story
I'm sure you will agree,
Don't bet on what you think
Will be a certainty.
'Cos the unexpected
It may happen,
And claim the victory.

JUST ME

What lies ahead
As I rise from my bed
Who today will I see?
No need to ask
There is after all, just me!

At the start of the day
Breakfast, what will it be?
No need to ask
There is after all, just me!

It's the start of the week
So what shall I seek
To accomplish a daily routine?
No need to ask
There is after all, just me!

No rain today, as yet
Get to the garden, maybe
But what shall I plant
Flowers, or maybe a tree?
No one to ask
There is after all, just me!

I may need to polish,
Or maybe to dust
I wonder what it will be?
No need to ask
After all, it's just for me!

After some brunch
Of biscuit, coffee or tea,
Lunch then to plan
I wonder, what's it to be?
There is after all, just me!

Still there's no rain, so,
Maybe a walk to the shop?
Then, back through the wood
No need to question,
There is after all, just me!

I get the odd caller
From home help or daughter,
Sure, they haven't a clue
That I wish they were you,
Instead of there being, just me.

The routine may vary,
But what's very scary
Is how to look forward, not back?
But no one to ask,
How to deal with that task
There is after all, just me!

I'm alone, but not lonely
After all, how could I be?
Not company I seek, but you,
But in my memory abiding
You ARE still here with me.

SEEKING

I was drawn to seek you
Wherever that might be,
Whether it was near at hand
Or far across the sea.

I was moved to find you
Your company I sought,
With love and understanding,
Some things just can't be bought.

You were sought among the hillsides
Among the fields so green
Between the trees and flowers
In sunshine or in rain
To seek, and maybe find you,
Much happiness to gain.

WAR

I wonder when,
I wonder if,
It may occur to man,
To make not bullets
Bombs, or missiles,
Instead to feed the hungry
Dry the children's tears,
And with each other, be reconciled

Why make war
When you could make peace?
Why cause pain
With eternal grief?
Better to agree to disagree,
Not force others to go and kill
Just to see things your way,
When we know, they never will.

GOING BACK

Unable to turn back the clock
No, no chance of that.
All those happy times
And sad times too, it seems
Are gone and only remembered
Within the house of dreams.

We cannot see the future
A good thing, that's for sure,
Unable to find out what it is
That hides behind life's door.
Go not back, nor forward
Gathering shadows, evermore.

Retracing your steps, no, no
I don't think it would be good.
Mistakes to rectify, my, my,
If only, if only, we could.
So just keep trying to do better
And do it as we should.

Follow the rails, follow the track
Over the bridges do follow,
Through tunnels so dark and deep
Straighten the bends, climb inclines steep
Looking only forward,
Unable to go back.

PAIN

I have a pain within my soul
It will not go away
I had that pain before we met
And then you came to stay.

All was well for many a year,
The pain no longer there,
But you were called and had to go
Then pain returned and no one seemed to care.

The emptiness where once you where
Is a reminder every day,
What that pain was like before
And will not go away.

But the joy that we had shared
Reminds me every day,
Your love it still surrounds me,
And will not go away.

LOST LOVE

Such deep, deep love
That cannot be erased
Although you are no longer here
Your love has all been saved.

You're always in my thoughts
My routine daily life,
And what still surrounds me
Are memories of you, my wife.

Time cannot remove
The bonds of many years,
But it would take a monsoon
To wash away the tears.

THINKING JUST OF YOU.

When I was asleep
I dreamed of you.
When I awoke,
I looked at you.
Making breakfast,
I made yours too.
When I was walking,
I thought of you.
When I was working,
I worked for you.
When I grew flowers,
They were for you.
All of my thoughts
They were for you.
Now you are gone,
But I must stay,
What can I do
To pass each day?
It is, to me very clear,
I will think of you, my dear,
As before, through all these years.

HEADSTONES

The headstones stand in lines
Like soldiers on parade,
Telling the names of those who've gone
And left this life's charade.

Is it sad, and is it right
To mention those gone before?
Gently to remind us
They are at heaven's door.

We never know exactly
And surely cannot tell,
Where it is they've gone to,
Which is probably just as well.

So the headstones mark the spot
Where human remains they wait,
While souls inside are freed
To enter heaven's gate.

BEGONE

Begone dark spirits of the night
Begone and stay away
Begone the ghosts that haunt the soul,
And welcome in the day.

Begone the haunting of the mind
Begone, begone I say
Give peace to daytime dreaming
That gently floats your way.

Release the darkness that surrounds
Your day of hopes and dreams
Begone to all the shadows
That from the sidewalk stream.

Begone to all the worries
Begone, begone I say
Don't sit alone in darkness
Let sunshine light your day.

Begone to ghostly spectres
Go far away from here,
With only brightness in your life
And show no sign of fear.

So dark spirits of the night
Begone again I say,
With angels to protect you
And guide you on your way.

WEATHER

Wind blows
Who knows
Whence it will go.

Sunny skies
Hurts the eyes,
Shades are needed.

Rain descends
Never ends
Floats the boats.

Thunder claps
Lightning snaps
Illuminates the sky.

Fog descends
Never mends
Where will it all go?

Frosty plains
Freezing rain,
Will it ever end?

Snowflakes fall
Covering all,
A silent eiderdown.

Sun kissed
Rain and mist
Wonder what will follow?

Weather changes
Through the ages
We must not intefere.

TRIBUTE TO CATHERINE.

Not just a wife,
Nor just a friend,
Not just a shoulder
Or a hand to just lend,
Not just an arm
On which to lean,
Nor just to do
What I wasn't keen
Not just to be eyes
When I couldn't see.
Yes, you were these things,
But much more, to me
My wife yes, my soulmate
My pal and my lover,
And to my children,
A loving, dear mother.

Ears that would listen
To my tale of woe,
To go somewhere for me
When I didn't want to go
All these things, you were to me,
Yes, and much more,
A voice in the darkness,
A hand I could hold
Someone to cuddle
When you said it was cold.

A gift of a lifetime
You were to me,
And when it was time
That you had to leave
I held you so tightly,
As you took your last breath
I hope that you're at peace
Wherever that may be,
And I'll pray for you daily
So please, don't forget me.

SPRINGTIME

Wintertime let's loose it's hold
As spring pops up its head,
The birds come out to sing,
Looking for a mate,
And forage round for food.

Now spring is come,
And that's a clue,
That slumber now is past
As wildlife starts to stir
A brand new life is cast.

All will awaken slowly,
From their winter sleep
With snowdrop and the crocus
And daffodils to follow,
Until the tulip becomes the focus.

The sun it starts to warm us
Lambs, they dance a jig
Skipping happily all about,
Leafy buds they break
To slowly open out.

Drowsy hedgehogs
From their slumber, still
Cautiously they venture
As, aware that often
There comes a sudden chill.

Don't venture out too soon
While winter chill is here,
Frost still covers all in white,
Moon lights up the darkness
On the clearest night.

Time enough to end your slumber
Just wait a little longer,
And with the mad march hare
Come out, the sun grows stronger,
Spring at last is here.

SHIPWRECKED

Marooned upon an island
Abandoned and forsake
Shipwrecked like a sailor
Life I must remake.

A castaway without you
In a tempestuous storm,
I need you here beside me
To love and keep me warm.

Change hopelessness to expectations
And seek to find a way,
To carry on without you
For I know you could not stay.

I'm marooned upon an Island
Separated from your hand,
Drifting ever outward
To find another land.

CLOUDS

A big black cloud hanging over me
Following wherever I go
To threaten and torment me
Why pursue me so?.

A big black cloud surrounding me
Hovering just above
That cloud can disappear as quick
When I remember love.

The big black cloud of darkness
On which then shines the light
Remembering your presence
And everything's alright.

REFLECTIONS

Reflect upon the reflection
Hold that in your heart,
Reflect upon the vision
That tears your soul apart.

Who knows in which direction
So look around and see ,
Or find out why reflection
Betrays your inner fear.

Look back at your achievements,
What is there to fear?
Past deeds to improve on
And all becomes more clear.

Reflection of our being
Can be a fruitful thing
Returning to reality,
Examining what we bring.

We are not the centre
Some may think we are,
We are just time travellers
Journeying to a star.

So reflect upon the journey
And where we may have been,
The next place that we go to
Is known alone to him.

TREASURE

Treasured beyond all measure
You were my perfect friend
Always there to help me,
My best pal to the end.

LOVE

Love is a thing of beauty
To treasure for all time
To hold this thing of beauty
Inside a world of grime.

No matter what the effort
Required to make it stand,
To hold us all together
Inside the mess of man.

I will hold you in my heart
No matter what the cost,
I'll defend my love whatever
That passion can't be lost.

Love is always timeless
Especially yours and mine
Defended and protected
Until the end of time.

SURPRISES

What awaits us today I wonder
To help, or maybe hinder,
Or just another soul,
Who passes by your window.

It maybe loud or maybe quiet
Who knows what it will be,
Every day holds surprises,
Let's just wait and see.

So bring it on, whatever
It surely has to be,
For a day without surprises
Would be a catastrophe.

A PLACE REMEMBERED

In that village quaint and quiet
I spent my younger years,
Like Rupert Brooke, in Grantchester.
Yes I grew up there, in Grantchester
And with his thoughts I do concur
The church clock, yes, still it stands
In Grantchester, in Grantchester.

Through Byrons wood, to Byron's pool
Was he, the Lord who went there
To bathe away from public stare
The cooling water to enjoy,
As did I, as a boy
But, like many others, further down
In shallow water, so you wouldn't drown.

In the mill pond, the water gushes
As underneath the bridge it rushes
To rejoin the lazy flow
Of the river down below,
To Cambridge, that academic city
With tree lined backs, and blossoms, pretty.

Grantchester is much a part
Of that academic town,
Distinguished wearers of the gown,
Come to the orchard to take tea
Scones with cream, jam and honey.
None of which would be complete
Unless sitting 'neath the trees to eat.

They tried, and failed,
To make a drama
A modern take on village life
In Grantchester, ah Grantchester.
Was no curate, just a vicar!
No detective great, nor villain vile,
Just some locals, who broke the stile
While crossing through the meadow.
Yes, a timeless place to be
If you grew up there, like me.
You just remember, I was there
A country life, without a care!

WHEN I'M THERE

Not sure where I'm going to
Or if I've been before,
Wherever it is, I'll soon know
And tell you when I'm there.

Not sure when I will go
Not sure just how soon,
Maybe it's somewhere near
Or the far side of the moon.

Not sure if it matters
Or if I really care
Maybe I will like it,
I'll tell you when I'm there.

Not sure what direction
Journey's end to find,
Maybe I'll just muddle on
And find out, when I'm there.

Not sure who'll be waiting
Anyone I knew?
Maybe lots, or maybe none
I'll tell you when I'm there.

May not want to be there
Seems we have no choice,
I'll tell you when I get there
You'll recognise my voice.

Not sure what to expect,
Whether it to dread,
I think it may be awesome
That vision in my head!

GUIDANCE

Guidance through life's corridors
Decisions we must make,
Paths to left,
Paths to right
Which one should we take?

Life's rich blend of choices
Inspire us,day or night
Listen to the voices
Questions to be asked,
With care, we'll be alright.

Who to give the answer,
With ourselves the final call,
In moments of deep thought
Invoke the spiritual wisdom,
Available to us all.

NIGHT SKY

The night sky
In illuminated splendour,
Provides us with a glimpse
Of what's beyond our eye.

More stars beyond our vision
Now lit by moon's reflection,
Those tiny dots of light
Show heaven's celestial might.

Our future,
It's out there somewhere,
In that vast expanse,
While in gravity, we dance.

Ever drifting, onward
Anchored in belief,
One day we just might get there
And find eternal relief.

So vast, it's but revealing
A little to our eye,
No matter what the season,
It leaves us wondering, why?

The night sky,
That vast expanse of space,
A huge, exciting distance
As on and on we race.

INVISIBLE

Don't ignore what isn't seen
For it doesn't mean it isn't there,
Don't give up on what's imagined
For what you think might be,
When you least expect it,
That's when you just might see,
The results of hesitating
Your opportunity is lost.
One day you will regret it
And soon will count the cost.

It may not yet be visible
To our human eye,
But we must be conscious
That time is passing by.
Be vigilant, be awake
The shadows hide a warning,
Of things, as yet unseen
The signs are there before us,
So think before you act,
That thing that isn't visible
Will keep you safe on track.

You cannot see the energy
That is magnetic force
But we all believe it,
And make use of it, of course.
To take it all for granted
With gratitude that's spurned,
By those who won't believe it
But really, we must respect
And give to what's invisible
Praise that has been earned.

HOLIDAYS IN WALES

When first we sought a place to go
With children- there were four,
So with our caravan safe in tow
Wales we went to tour.

The better half had planned it,
And found a place surreal,
Near to sea and beaches
Porthmadog, it seemed ideal.

Just a short step to town
But a rural idyll, it was that,
With shops, for chips and icecreams
And antique shops where we could chat.

That first visit was a heatwave
Water was scarce indeed,
But, in Jones the farmer's field
We relaxed to play and read.

We walked along to the beach
Took half an hour, at most
Down along the harbour path
Watching boats along the coast.

The church along up the hill
We went each time we stayed,
And listened to the singing
As Fr Micheal prayed.

Wonderful those visits were
We went there, summertime and more
Later bringing our two young girls
To add to children four.

When the eldest, they moved on
With the three youngest we still went
Slept in van like gipsies
With Steven, in a tent.

Those visits they continued
For many years, they played,
Still we went there often
To visit friends they'd made.

The years produced a contact
With antiques, I went to trade,
Would go there for the day
Hoping a profit could be made.

Those holidays, they made a memory
So much so, one married there,
Beneath the snowdon mountain
They pledged each other's care.

All of us are grateful still
For lifetime memories made,
None of us will yet forget
As in the sea we wade.

Most of all , as we all know
The one no longer here
Was she who picked the spot
And fixed the lifelong glow.

ENVY

Envy not the rich
And pity not the poor,
Because if you've found love
You have riches, galore.

Don't wish for more to have
Nor waste your life in gloom,
But if you have love,
You've found nuggets on the moon.

Wish not for riches
Or things you haven't got,
Because if you've got love
You have the midas touch.

Wish not for power
Or glory, in this world,
Have love and enjoy it,
Your banner is unfurled.

RACING

Life is like a horse race
The fences we must jump,
No time to dodge the ditches
We scramble to the front.

Out of breath we puff,
Out of time, we rush
No time to pause or wait,
As to the front we push.

So often we forget
As round the bend we finish
Those who get there first,
Have seen their time diminish.

So take your time,
Be gentle round that bend,
Don't let time pursue you
Run steady to the end.

CANDLEGLOW

A little candle, glowing
A light of hope,
A light for peace,
A light to keep us going
A comfort in the night,
To calm your nerves
To quell all fears
To know you'll be alright.

Now two candles burning,
One for you, one for me,
To inspire you, and protect
Keep us steadfast, just to see
Show the spirit in reflection
Showing where you need to be,
Little candle, do not flicker
Burn for all eternity.

Now a dozen candles flutter
Gently murmuring in the breeze,
Brightly how they shine around us
Symbols of both hope and peace
Joining with the prayers of angels,
In praises which will never cease.

As many as the stars above us
So many now the candles burn,
Each a sign of light, eternal
Burn little candles, show the way
That keeps us always in your name,
To feel the protection, and the hope
Which burns in that eternal light
From just a flicker, to a flame.

Each day light your candle
Watch it gently burn,
Glowing gently through the darkness
Knowing that it will not fade,
Through all kinds of hardship
Burn little candle, light the way,
Remind us, there is always hope
Burn through night and into day.

The candle, is such a simple thing
But oh, the comfort, warmth and solace,
That humble candle will us bring.
With the glow our prayers united
When so many burn as one,
Say a prayer, a soul departed
With angelic choirs to sing,
Light, to mend the broken hearted.

TIME, THE MASTER

Time is a relentless master
Closing down yesterday
And opening up tomorrow
Pushing forward, ever onward
No hesitation, just persuasion
Of all that has to be,
Time, the relentless master.

For good or bad, no delay
Time, fast cruising ever forward,
No change of speed, no indeed
Time, the unseen, unforgiving
Time, you are the master.

DAWN

The sun peeps up it's sleepy head
Dispels the night time mist
The birds start up their daily song
The grass by sunbeams kissed.

An eerie silence broken now
Firstly by the blackbirds song,
Then the song thrush, and the robin
Others,they all sing along.

What a welcome to the daytime
Natures happy wake up call
A relaxing way to slowly stir
A brand new day to welcome all.

DUSK

As the daytime sunbeams rest
The birds return unto the nest,
The crows, on tree tops tall
Squabbling madly to get their place
Every night, the same old race.

Those tree tops, suddenly are still
Other birds, they slowly hush,
Until at last no sound is heard.
Oh, to have the sense and wisdom
Of a humble, feathered bird.

The daylight now is fading
The evening sparrow mesmerising
Cling together, slowly quietening,
The crows in tree tops crowded
Jostling, the sound of fighting.

Lofty tree tops are silent now
With nests that cradle in the bough,
Dusk now brings a quiet and so
Hastened on by growing dimness ,
The feathered chatter gives way to stillness.

SUMMER IN THE PARK

Sunshine peeps through broken clouds
Warming up the daylight hours,
Before more heavy summer showers.
Thunder rumbles in the distance
With the threat of more to follow,
The flowers, in raindrops glisten
Wind, it's pace doth quicken,
Couples hasten from the park
Long before before the hours of dark,
Not willing to get more soaking
The dog, it just needs walking!
Children reluctant, protesting loudly
While daylight it still seems abounding,
But thunder rumbling out a warning
And heavy raindrops start a"splattering,
What a wonder, what a colour
As lightning gives way to thunder.
Take some shelter if you dare
But under trees, do take care,
It has been known to be a danger
So, explained the parkside ranger,
Should lightning strike the tree,
What would become of me?
Better make off, as you are
Try to make it to the car,
And having made the dash
Go to the chippy, dad's got the cash!

SEARCH FOR A DREAM

The day begins
Without much hope,
And ends
Inside a dream.

Today's the day
To see the way,
Reflecting,
And maybe dream.

Today is lit
By sunshine bright,
Don't end
Without a dream.

Today's the day
It just might be,
Perhaps,
To have a dream.

Today is here
So don't forget
To always
Want to dream.

Reality is harsh
And always so
If not,
We wouldn't dream.

Start the day
In just the way
You want,
But end it, in a dream.

So don't let's waste
Or end in haste,
Together,
In a dream.

They think I'm mad
But I'm glad
I found in you,
My dream.

POLITICIANS

There was a politician once,
Who thought that he was smart
Indeed, he was, could get a diploma
If lying was an art!

Most, they look for recognition,
Others look for power,
None would get much income
If we paid them by the hour.

Some, of course, they try hard
To change things for the best,
But they get put down, held back
By the rabble, that's the rest!

DAYDREAMING

I sit and quietly ponder
Gazing at the sky
Seeing grey clouds yonder
Letting time just drift on by.

Lost inside sweet memories
With thoughts surrounding you
Life is so much harder
Without you in it too.

Bright skies or black clouds,
They matter not to me
Life can be overwhelming
When it's you I cannot see.

Cheer up your voice says clearly
Fond memories we still share
Just gaze into the sunset
And know I'm always there.

FRIENDSHIP

Good friends make life worthwhile
They cheer you up
And make you smile,
Give you hugs
When you feel down,
Lend a hand, when it's needed
Listen carefully
Your troubles, heeded.

Good friends will know
And have no doubt,
If they're in need
You'll help them out,
And when all problems
Have been solved
Friends stay with you
'Till you're old.

When all is well, and time to spare
You'll have a barbie
Without a care,
'Cos all through life
It's ups, it's downs
Through joys and troubles
Which you share,
You know your friends,
Are always there.

MR. PIGEON

Out of my window
I can see
A giant conifer,
Tall as tall, as tall can be,
Perched at the top, looking down
A family of pigeons
Can see me frown,
For these pigeons
They're a pest,
They sit on my rooftop
And just make a mess.
I am thinking, how delicious
A scrumptious pigeon pie would be!
Mister pigeon, villainous thug
Is looking down
And feeling smug.
He is thinking, without a doubt
If I went closer
He'd bomb me out!
I hate that pesky pigeon lot
They conspire and coo
To hatch a plot,
If I had my way
I'd have them shot.
That's very cruel
Some would say
So I doubt, very much
That I'll get my wish
To put them pigeons
In a dish!

THE APPARITION

Was at the stroke of midnight
The ghost, it first appeared,
I thought I must be dreaming
And when I woke, the apparition disappeard.

But no, that ghost had come to haunt me
And that ghost, it did not rest,
It's shrieks and constant wailing,
It haunted with such zest.

I thought that it would melt away
As darkness passed to dawn
And sunshine warmed the day,
But no, it carried on, wailing, so forlorn.

As sunbeams show a lazy smile,
That ghost, it will surely banish,
So, with all the strength I had,
I willed the spirit, vanish!

Then, all at once, it was quiet,
Nothing to be heard,
Maybe, just maybe, a dream?
A ghost, really! How absurd.

I wondered, what it could mean
What did the spirit say?
Was it something I had done
That took my breath away.

Was it here to tell me,
Of something I must change?
Whatever it is, I'll do it
No more please,
That spectre strange.

That night of fear, now long past
Reminds me, growing old
That spectre, when I think of it
It makes my blood run cold.

A GRANNY IN THE GARDEN

We've got a granny
Who lives in the shed,
A log cabin, (begging pardon),
Built at the bottom of our garden.

It all came to be
Most unexpectedly,
We built this log cabin
Just like I said,
And granny took a fancy
To live in this shed.

I could live in here, she said
Yes, I fancy a shed
At the bottom of the garden.
With the fairies to dwell,

Dad shook his head,
It didn't bode well.

What could we say,
She moved in that day,
Took all her stuff,
Although it was tough,
She made it look cosy,
For her, life was rosy.

It might get too cold
Now that you're old, we said,
But not at all, not at all,
I'll put up some pictures
To decorate the wall,
Said granny, as she hopped into bed.

Our granny, she said
I like this 'ere shed!
We said, give it a week
She'll move out right quick
If she gets a bit sick,
Months later, and granny's still there.

We've got a granny in the shed
At the bottom of the garden,
Outside she grows flowers
Not a weed to be seen,
And a mat that says "welcome"
She keeps it so tidy and clean.

We're not too sure
What to put on the door,
Is it a home, or a shed?
Yes, granny lives in the garden
In a fairy dell, and as far we can tell
She likes it right well !

We've got a granny in the garden
She lives alone in the shed,
Only time it will tell,
If it's a good place to dwell
Just her, in the shed,
With a chair, a book, and a bed.

WHO AM I ?

Tell me who I am?
Spirit or a man,
Tell me, tell me please,
Tell me who I am.

Tell me who I was,
Whom I meant to be,
Tell me, tell me please
Tell me what you see.

Tell me what to be
Where to go
Who to see,
Tell me who I am.

Tell me who I am
Cloud or spirit,
Ghost or shadow?
Tell me who I am.

The great mystery of man,
Tell me, tell me do,
Tell me, tell me if you can,
Apparition, vision, or a man.

THE VESSEL

The body is just the vessel
For the soul to live within,
But the wickedness of man
Conceals the eye from sin.

The wise among us mortals
Look beyond that cage
Containing the mean or gracious,
As we mature with age.

The wisdom of king solomon
Knew to look in depth,
To see the truest nature,
The saint or just a wretch.

Those whose heart is truest
Know to look inside
At the true intentions,
That evil tries to hide.

Your generosity and kindness,
Are witnessed as we look
Deep into the heart and mind
Whichever path we took.

MEMORY

To catch a memory

Inside the folds of time,

Shake it up

Dust it down,

And make it

Yours and mine.

Printed in Great Britain
by Amazon